Proof or Conse

A HUMOROUS LOOK AT TYPOS, MISSPELLINGS, WRONG WORDS, AND MISPLACED PUNCTUATION

by SUSAN M. LOVETT

ILLUSTRATED BY ARI SCOTT

SML
PROOFREADING

Proof
or
Consequences!™

Enjoy!
Sue Lovett

Published by SML Proofreading
       sml-proofreading.business.site
       smlproofreading@gmail.com

Manufactured in the United States of America

ISBN: 978-0-578-81744-6

Cover and interior page design and layout by Stephen Tiano / stephen@stephentianobookdesign.com

All illustrations by Ari Scott / ari.scott1212@gmail.com

This book is dedicated to my grandfather, Walter Clark and my mother, Marion Clark Lovett, who passed their "Clark humor" down to me.

Acknowledgments

I am extremely grateful to Steve Tiano for his expert design and layout as well as his professional patience working with this amateur.

It took me a while to find an illustrator, but when Ari Scott was sent my way, I discovered I had an absolute gem. Her drawings and enthusiasm kept me laughing and smiling.

Thanks must go to Carol M., who kept me from ever backing down with this idea, constantly telling me, "I can't wait to read it!"

Thanks to Felicia Garant for contributing to my collection of clippings and being supportive of my project.

Special thanks to Stephen Sterns and M.L. Buchman for answering so many of my questions and getting me going in the right direction.

Much appreciation to Tom Miller for his helpful ideas and suggestions and for being one of my biggest cheerleaders.

Thanks, too, to Mindy H. for all the exchanges of ideas and references as we've traveled similar paths.

And gratitude to the members of the Editorial Freelancers Association (EFA) discussion list who were so generous with their answers to my questions or recommending others who could help me if they couldn't.

scuttling it. And this being ▮▮▮▮▮▮ and all, he passed word around the waterfront that any equipment remaining on the boat was there for the picking.

"So, the local pirates descended," ▮▮▮▮▮ said. "Someone got a wench. Somebody else took the boom. Somebody got a radio antenna and some tools."

The stripping of th▮

I bet it was the first guy there who grabbed the wench!

and I, too, felt like a monster.

But this all changed once I held my son for the first time. I can't imagine now living without my little guy, and I wouldn't change him for the world.

And you can smell them coming a mile away!

First we'll work on the grocery list,
then we'll do the "Honey Do" list ...

Woman out of hospital after jumping from car

southbound near Exit 20.

████████ landing on the payment also triggered a multi-car crash when drivers from Lynn and North Reading swerved to avoid hitting her while she lay in the road.

I hope it was for a really large amount! She's going to need it!

The challenges faced by the fishing industry, ███████ school officials and families and the other stories cited among the top sagas of 2013 were hardly the only ones we all confronted over the last 12 months.

From a 20-year blizzard to.

. . .

Whew! Even RUDOLPH wouldn't have been able to get through THAT!

13

The Fire Department's ambulance squad also responded, but ▮▮▮ reused treatment at the scene. Police

*Nothing like recycled treatment
to make you better!*

15

▶ Weather
Snow tampering off in afternoon. Three to six inches.
High, 31°; low, 8°.
Forecast: marine, Page 7; extended Page 24.

Don't mess around with snow;
you never know how much you'll get!

...ing a Democrat who takes office on Jan. 21, also announced the creation of a task force within the attorney general's office to help sharpen the response to the rug abuse problem in the state.

"Every day, families across Massachusetts are being torn apart by this epidemic."

A call for the Carpet Police!

perspective.
"Those of you who know the film 'Cacablanca' may remember the last line: 'I think this is the beginning of a beautiful friendship,'" he said. "Th...

White poop??

work on the measure, known
as Amendment 23, pouring
over the full range of alter-
natives now expected to be
presented to the council for

Thursday, March 10

11:13 a.m.: A hazardous situation was reported regarding a beer truck with an open rear end on Summer Street.

Nope, don't want to try to picture that!

21

Now in recovery for almost four years, ███ works for the ████████-████ Organization for Addition Recovery (██████) to advocate for improved addiction treatment and recovery support services.

Subtraction recovery is next.

Would that be Mojave? Sahara?
Sounds kind of dry ...

DATE 11/03/2017 FRI
CARDS/STATIONARY T1 $3.25
TAX1 AMT $0.20
TOTAL $3.45
CASH $4.00
CHANGE $0.55
NO.022724 REG01 REGISTER-1 TIME 16:12

Looks like those cards aren't going anywhere!

Basic Math II

██████, not eligible for free agency until after the 2012 season, batted a major league-best .359 with 32 homers and 100 RBIs last year, continuing his resurgence following cocaine and alcohol addition. He missed much of the last month of the

*You're sure to improve
after adding cocaine and alcohol.*

2/8 at 9:39 a.m. A ~~Blackstrap~~ Road resident reported a suspicious vehicle was parked in her driveway and several men were walking around. Police reported the women forgot the men were from a gutter company she reportedly hired to work on her home.

She must've gotten her mind out of the gutter.

■ Police notified the Department of Public Works of snow-covered roads throughout the town Tuesday at 10:30 p.m. Monday.

Roads were still slick into

Someone has a crystal ball?

water, I wanted to do some-
thing in ████████. That's
the first big hurtle. I spoke
with a restaurateur who

*Sounds like a big jump
for Yertle the Turtle!*

*Dr. Seuss, 1958

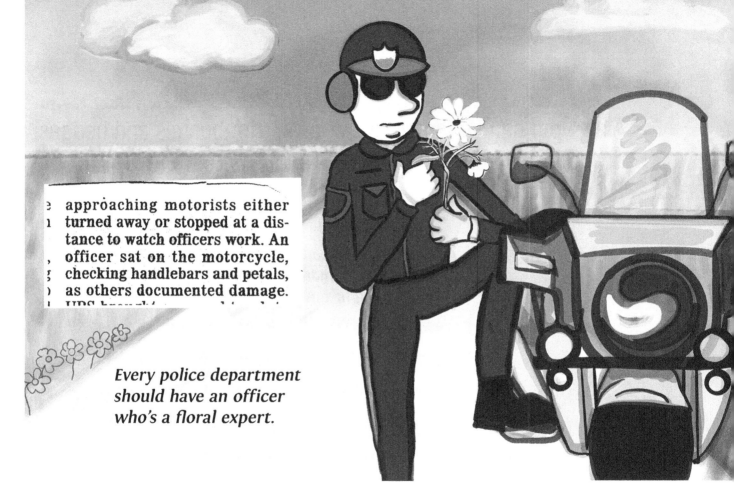

approaching motorists either
turned away or stopped at a dis-
tance to watch officers work. An
officer sat on the motorcycle,
checking handlebars and petals,
as others documented damage.

*Every police department
should have an officer
who's a floral expert.*

Also, your handyman will mow laws, trim bushes and hedges, do odd jobs, furniture repairs, chairs, etc. Please call the

You don't like that law?
Your handyman will just
mow it right down for you!

uncorrectable vision loss among seniors.

- Protect your eyes from the sun's damaging ultraviolet rays by wearing UV-raged sunglasses.

- Have your eyes checked annually if you have diabetes, high blood pressure, a family history of

The latest in angry eyewear.

■ A telephone pole behind the police station also sparked with fire Thursday about 5:10 p.m., but the rain tampered out any flames and ████ ███ responded to repair the pole, police said.

Don't mess with the rain, either!

cautioned residents to take preventative action by repairing window screens, using netting on baby carriages, wearing long sleeves and pants during peek mosquito hours- between dusk and dawn- and also dumping and

Don't look now, but that just might be a mosquito!

roof. The disconnect leaves a gap between the building's walls and roof's edge, and through that gap insulation peaks out and occasionally birds swoop past the browned fluff to visit it

Visitors to ~~█████████~~ waterfront Thursday evening got a peak at a special weekend visitor.
The Tall Ship Pieter Castle, c

granite stones. Just floating away, sails flapping, sneaking a peak up at the seagull nests over the hill as the gulls wheel and spin

My curiosity has been piqued,
but I'm feeling a bit peaked.

out of jail after battery charge

Didn't realize you could be jailed if your car wouldn't start!

Checked out

4/9 at 12:01 p.m. A resident contacted police to report her purse was missing after a trip to the grocery store. A few days later, she contacted police to report her purse had been found, in her grocery bags.

Fire calls

Sure hope she hadn't bought any frozen items! (Of course, that would lead to cold cash . . .)

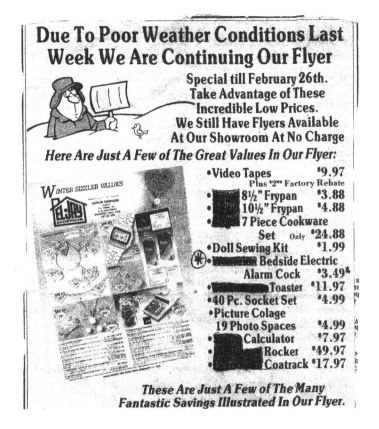

Does it get YOU up? Or do you get IT up?

The four ████████ City Hall towers are not just decorative architectural elements, but they serve as part of 19th century building's ventilation system, which is now back in working order, letting hot air out of city hall.

That's one way
to do it!

According to police reports, an intoxicated white male in his 30s or 40s and wearing a short-sleeved beige short with a pink handkerchief around his

Wednesday, March 20

6:31 p.m.: A resident came into the station to report his Social Security number had been comprised, and fraud committed. Police are investigating.

My social security number is comprised, too— of nine numbers!

44

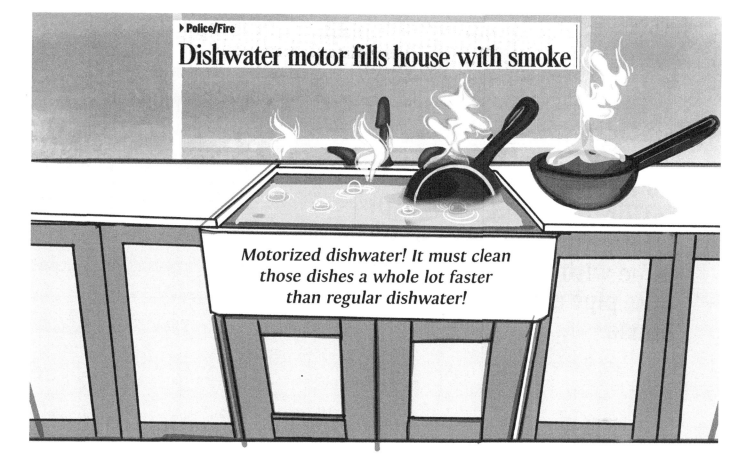

speeding.

6:15 p.m.: Fire alarm activation on ▓▓▓▓▓▓ Hill. Firefighters discovered an issue with the home's stove flute pipe and ventilated the house.

Does it play "Home on the Range"?

The increased risk of disease, however, has increased their already thorough cleaning regiment.
"We have been doing it all along,

■ ████████ ████, 4, of ██ ████████., Rockport, had a charge of assault and battery dismissed due to a failure to prosecute. ████ was charged in February after police allege that she assaulted a woman at her ████████ home.

1:08 a.m.: ████████ ████, 2, of ████████ Rockport, is facing charges of operating under the influence of alcohol, negligent operation of a motor vehicle, and failing to stay within marked lanes after he was involved in a crash on ████ Avenue.

Saturday, July 20

Boy! They're starting everything
younger and younger
these days!

■ A █████████ resident called police at 5:16 p.m. Saturday to report that someone had broken into his home and stolen his green beans from the refrigerator. The man said he wanted a report on file.

Must've been a vegetarian!
Or the Jolly Green Giant?

"We brought Tiger back to our condo and the next day took him to the vet for treatment," ████████ said. "Luckily, he was not hurt badly, but he was riddled with parasites, ticks and flees.

If I were covered with ticks and parasites, I'd run away, too!

The younger ▮▮▮▮▮ was arrested last month after police say he urinated at ▮▮▮▮▮ Field while Pee Wee football practice was going on. Police say ⌐

"Pee Wee"—well, what does that bring to YOUR mind?

In other words, this is   li
undo stress on the manager.   ‹
Spring training is sup-

Stress has an "undo" option?
Sign me up!

After graduating from RHS, he served in the Navy in the Koran war. Upon his return,

It's not kosher to fight over a religious book.

55

Avenue that had an unlocked door. During the chase, police used the K9 ███, who mistakenly bit two officers —one on the backside, one on the thigh — but also bit ███ in the confusion.

Which part of the body is the "confusion"?

Officers responded to ⌐ Road and ▮▮▮▮ Street after a resident called to report an injured duck in the road at 7:59 p.m. Friday. The duck turned out to be a dog, and was not injured.

Maybe it was a duckshund?

on Earth. He left the circus in 1988 to teach, leading high students through the intricacies of chemistry, algebra and physics.

Science and math are SO much easier to understand while high!

cey Boulevard last August.

████, meanwhile, covered the story as the city stepped up its efforts in the drug fight through, among other things, providing Narcan, a nasal spray administered to revere the effects of a drug overdose.

I really don't think ANYONE admires and respects the effects of a drug overdose.

11:24 p.m.: A [redacted]
Circle resident reported seeing someone enter a neighbor's house via a doggy door. According to police, the man who used the doggy door was the homeowner. He told officers he didn't have his keys on him at the time.
Some days are ruff like that.

its needed local permits by the City Council, involves a potential delay in the start of a $7 infrastructure improvement of the

What are we talking about here? A LEGO® infrastructure?

FATTOUSH

What you end up with when you eat too much.

Elementary School student ▊▊▊▊, left, looks into a chute and watches as his apple gets ground up in an apple cider press along with ▊▊▊ ▊▊▊▊ of the Food Project, who donated the use of the press for the school's Harvest Day on Friday.

I think I'll just pass on that apple cider, thank you.

64

She was member of ███████ ██ ███ ███ and was their first female exulted ruler in the lodge history. She cher- ished he tim spent the

Everyone was overjoyed at the election of their first female leader.

65

Police surround the Rehabilitation Center in ▮▮▮▮▮▮▮▮, Florida. Nine elderly patients died after being kept inside a nursing home that turned into a sweatbox when Hurricane Irma kn via AP, Focked out its air conditioning for three days.

Those focked out air conditioners can be deadly!

A woman
who found a
lump on her
breast called
her doctor,
and went in
for a mam-
mography. She was diag-

Is that like wanting your picture taken and going in for a photography?

On Brady and Belichick

The bands played, shoppers shopped and the boats went out for, respectively, the ███████ Country Fest, the Festival by the Sea, and the Bluefin Blowout.

The boats went out Thursday night for the Blowfin Blueout in ███████ and by the close of the event Saturday, 16 tuna had been

Is a Blowfin Blueout a Bluefin Blowout turned inside out?

mid-sized, secondary anchor group — ▬ Hardware, ▬ Store and ▬ — is a solid row, except for a vagrancy at the western end.

In the center, ~~~~

That western end COULD present a problem.

ately closed around him. They returned all that protection, love and sunshine that ▮ had given. What ye sew, so shall ye reap.

Does that include buttons?

73

U.S. Army veteran ███████████ sang the Star Spangled Banner followed by a melody of patriot songs.

Or possibly even a medley of patriotic songs!

12:41 p.m.: A caller reported that a male driver struck his vehicle, got out, threw his shoes and shirt into the street and began turning cartwheels down the street before running into some backyards off ███████ ████ Road. Police searched but could not locate the man. Officers are investigating.

Piece of Junk!

5:29 p.m.: The Fire Department responded to a fire alarm at Highview Road, but it was just that the flu had not been opened all the way on the fireplace.

Just trying to avoid catching a virus!

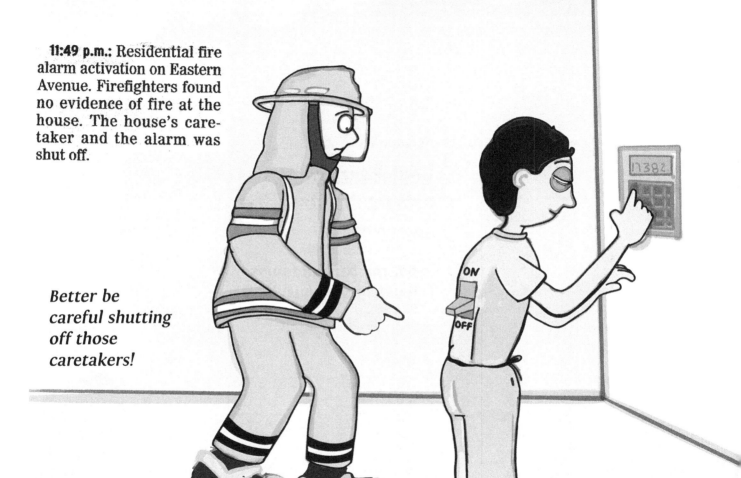

11:49 p.m.: Residential fire alarm activation on Eastern Avenue. Firefighters found no evidence of fire at the house. The house's caretaker and the alarm was shut off.

Better be careful shutting off those caretakers!

s or Cape Ann.

Legislature sets
ales tax holiday

ROSTON

*Bet the bars and pubs
will be really busy!*

Street. ███ ███████ Auto Clinic was called to tow the car out. Once freed, the car was able to drive away from the scene on its own power.

Tuesday, April 2

n   8:14 p.m.: A suspicious vehi-
y   cle was reported to be parked
ı   at Clammers Beach. It was
    two people in their car eat-
    ing Chipotle who then went
    on their way.

    6:05 p.m.: A tow truck driver

Just can't get enough of that stuff!

right, and ~~[redacted]~~ work on crosses and alter breads at ~~[redacted]~~ home last week.

~~[redacted]~~

But those breads were fine just the way they were!

State. A priest took him under his wings and made ▮▮▮ an accolade, when he was young. In later years, he loved

morning.

Tuesday, Oct. 2
10:16 a.m.: A woman on ███ ███ Avenue reported two dogs ran inside her house. Animal control told the woman to open her doors so the dogs would run back outside.
11:25 a.m.: Report of

Why didn't I think of that?

Stolen by a fiddler crab, no doubt!

Birds Eye Viola!
9 Varieties

Everyday Low Price

3⁹⁹

21 oz. PKG.

Pagoda

Ah! THAT's where that instrument ended up!

was closely involved in that decision.

Instead of filing a federal complaint, ███-
████ appealed to the state Civil Service
Commission, which overseas such appoint-
ments. He also filed a discrimination complaint with the Massachusetts Commission

*Sorry, but you'll have to travel across the water
to file THAT complaint!*

supper.

"That is about $700 verses $7,000," ████████ said. "It is ridiculous."

Other restaurants closi for a tim

Huh. Maybe I should start writing poetry. Looks rather lucrative!

Workers put on the diminishing touches on the main altar and stage as preparations for St. Peter's Fiesta are put into high gear. The festivities will kick off Wednesday evening with the opening of the carnival and close Sunday.

Can't have that altar
TOO fancy, after all!

**Right: A group
of musicians
with horns, play
Hey Jude by the
Beetles as other
musicians emerge
for the crowd to
form a flash mob
during Motif Day.**

Next group up: The Ladybugs!

In the other half of the newly renovated Town Hall, librarians and volunteers bustled around stalking the shelves.

Isn't that illegal?

DEAL of the DAY

Free tire air refreshener

Page 7

HUH?

FREE TREE AIR FRESHENER

~~████████████~~ *OHHH!*

CAR WASH

~~████████████~~

~~████████████~~

Offer good on 3/12/11 and 3/13/11 only.
Rules: One coupon per family per visit.
No photocopies accepted.

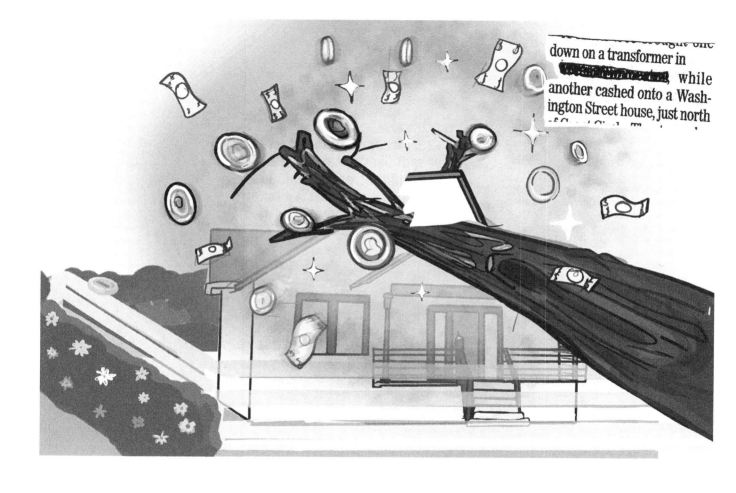

down on a transformer in ██████████████, while another cashed onto a Washington Street house, just north

a.m. Firefighters found a puddle of split disinfectant on a floor in the building, and recommended that the bank call a cleaning company to remove it.

DISIN FECTANT

Maybe they should call that regiment.

■ ▓▓▓▓▓▓▓, 26, of ▓▓ ▓▓▓▓▓▓ Ave. was charged with fraudulent use of electricity. -The charge was continued without a finding until December, she was ordered

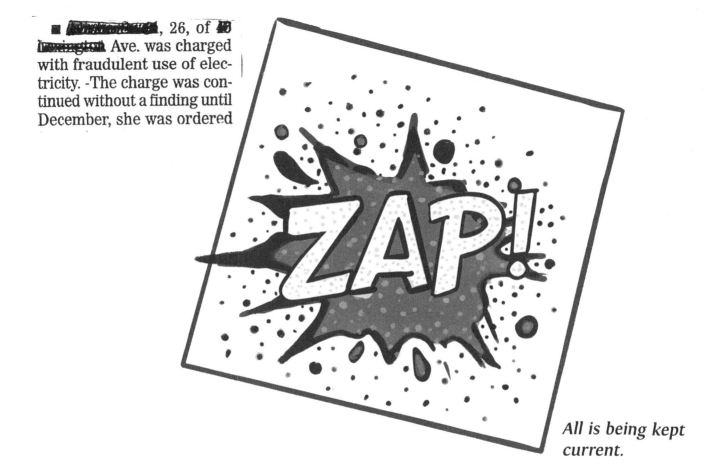

All is being kept current.

The ultimate workplace sin: Emails with explanation points!

To: Bossdude@abcco.com
From: workerdude@abcco.com

- *Well, I did this because . . .*
- *I did that for this reason . . .*
- *I thought that needed . . .*

▮▮ shuts down Angles, ▮▮ take series

Would that be right angles? Obtuse?

across the waves, as small children snuck from their beds, crept up to the windows, crouching down to not be detected, to watch

Married folks and widowers won't do.

103

Friday, April 2

1:05 p.m.: A ███████████ resident reported loose baby squirrels in their back yard.

Be careful where you step! What WERE those squirrels eating, anyway?

A dirty story indeed!

Longtime fishermen and boat owner ▮▮▮▮▮ said the $30,000 grants received for the three fishing corporations that own his F/V ▮▮▮▮, F/V ▮▮▮▮▮▮ and F/V ▮▮▮▮▮▮, pictured, will allow him to rehire crewmen he laid because of the COVID-19 pandemic.

Drastic times call for drastic measures

9:58 a.m.: A loose dog was reported in the middle of Martin Street and making its way to the police station, possibly to turn itself in.

• LEWISTON — A Lewiston man apparently attempting to flee police was arrested after he was discovered hiding in a stall in a rest room at ████████ General Hospital.

████████████████████████████████████, Lewiston, was flushed out of his hiding spot by police and arrested on a superior court warrant charging him with burglary and theft, according to police spokesmen.

Urine a lot of trouble...

facts sufficient to warrant a
guilty finding and had her
case continued without a
funding until April 2016 on
a charge of resisting arrest.
She was also ordered t

Case continued?
No funding
for you!

"Al, and our other cider makers, are constantly testing," ~~said~~ said, sitting at a natural wood bar with dim, warm lightning filling the space.

I'm struck by the electric ambiance!

██████████ was charged in July after a vehicle reported stolen from Walpole crashed into a utility police in ████████. ████████ was the passenger in the vehicle according to police reports.

Being utility police is a dangerous job!

~~...drive home with it.~~

A utility police on the corner of ████ Lane and ████████ Road was struck sometime before 8:00 a.m. Tuesday. Police have no suspects, National Grid reparied the pole.

Should be safer now that the pole's "reparied" though.

Among its features are a gallery area, enclosed head and a bow-gate with rungs in the front that lower into the water to afford easy access.

Who WOULDN'T want an area for artwork on their boat?

and mental health issue. It was a slow dissent, crossing more boundaries each time," she said.

Just say "No!"

Police probe theft of tables from rail yard

By ████████
STAFF WRITER

ROCKPORT – Rockport police are investigating missing cables that were reportedly stolen Friday from the ████'s commuter rail yard, police said.

Awww . . . and we were going to have a picnic, too!

An employee of ███████████████s and ████████ mascot ██████████ offer free samples of ████████s New England Style Stuffed Clams to the crows at the July 23 ██████ ████████ tennis match at the ██████████ Athletic Club.

Those lucky birds!

areas."

Although the parking ban was lifted as of 8 p.m. Sunday, ███ urged drivers to do all they can to avid impeding further snow removal operations.

That ⸺

If you're going to do wrong, do so vigorously!

But at what cost? This project does not factor in the neighborhood's loss of privacy or its safety, or its fragile salt march environment. It does not accept or address the ~~~~~~

Fragile salt on the move!

■ A ███████ man reported finding a "suspicious vile" containing a white powder substance in a hallway bathroom at the Inn at ███████ at 9:20 a.m. Tuesday.

And I have a vial suspicion about this!

won the fourth-place prizes, picketing $1,000 each.

The fifth-place prizes of

Protesting is lucrative? Who'd've guessed?

PUT ME IN COACH

What's the matter?
You don't like first class?

and a niece ███████████ He
was the also the grandfather
of the late ████████████ formerly of Rowley and bother of
the late ████████ formerly
of Essex.

*Siblings DO often find
one another a nuisance!*

A woman called police at 8:50 a.m. Monday to report that her dog was being chased by angry beavers.

The woman said she had

Dam those beavers, anyway!

Department officials at 5:40 p.m. on Monday when they received a call from ███- ██ Medical Associates. The town resident was transported to ██████ Hospital with stroke-like systems.

■ ▀▀▀

All systems aren't go.

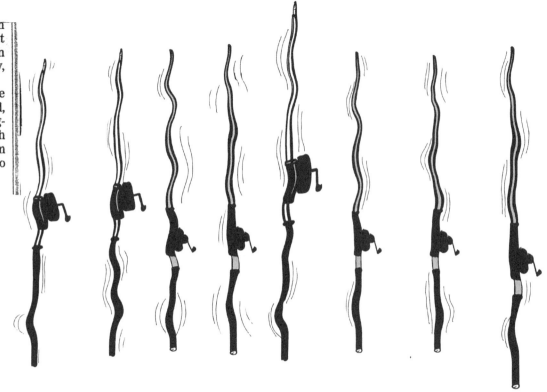

Aside from the fact that this man had stolen fishing equipment in his possession . . .

127

Gloucester.

[redacted] was exciting Grant Circle onto Route 128 when officers observed her vehicle swerving, according to a police report. The offi-

It doesn't pay to get a rotary excited!

Woman reports rail station theft

OUTSDOORS: Wookcock hunting season

Half Wookie, half rooster?

OUTDOORS: The Russed Grouse is nest in spring

At first she catches

Maybe a Russian bird?
Headline sounds a little Russian . . .

— A Western Avenue went to the police station Monday morning to report that numerous bottles and cans have been dumped on his property for the past several weeks. . .

Watch out! Western Avenue on the move! Could Eastern Avenue be next?

DOCK: Meeting to be help tomorrow

Looks like someone needs help TODAY!

boat from New Jersey, headed into the ████████ Marina when, the Coast Guard said, it ran around on some rocks along the ████████ Break-water Monday night.

Was the boat named Sue?
A rocky relationship
for shore.

cie, police indicated.

■ A ▮▮▮▮▮▮▮▮ Avenue man reported to police at 10:26 a.m. Monday that someone had stolen an iPod andewww a prescription bottle of Oxycodone from his unlocked car overnight

The thief wasn't the writer of this report, was he?

First Run

Landscape & Landscaping
"Start 2012 In The Green"

Hiring individuals with valid Ma Drivers License
Maintenance Crews & Landscape Construction.
Health--Dental--Affleck--401K Fax ~~978-012-1020~~
~~emailjobs@ralphlandscaping.com~~

Doesn't say whether it's Ben or Casey.
Maybe you get a choice.

■ Two Labradors attacked a flock of seven domestic chickens at 3 p.m. Monday. Animal control is looking for two of the chickens. Police said the owner had given names to each of the chickens, though offices were unable to provide them.

Bob? Carol? Ted? Alice? Moe? Larry? Curly?

— Police received a report of loose chickens on Dodge Street Friday about 9:21 a.m.

Police went to look for the chickens, but officers could not confirm Friday whether the chickens were still wandering in the area, or had flown the coop.

Maybe they crossed the street to Main!

to report an outage.

■ At 5:19 p.m. Saturday, a chicken crossed the road on Main Street. The chicken's owner was notified, and the owner was able to catch the chicken and remove it from the street.

It apparently got to the other side safely—but we still don't know why!

139

property in the home.

■ Police are investigating reports that a boy punched a 14 year old girl in the face twice during an alteration on Mansfield

He altered her face?
Arrest the bully!

Then came tragedy, when
two jet-liners crashed into
both towers of New York's
World Trade Center, another
into The Pentagon, and a
third slammed into a field in
Pennsylvania.

How many planes was that?

Poor Clarence Birdseye, reduced to an avian orb.

Cumberland fee hike forces older clammers to shell out

Bet you they clamored about it!

A dolphin showing clear signs of distress in shallow water off Davis Neck on Sunday night will likely die, according to experts, but its death would probably bare no significance to the population.

"We're excited for our staff to get this recognition for our own or original programming and content, but we're also proud of members, who come in her and do their own work and have now won awards as well."

Bleep! Censored! X-rated!

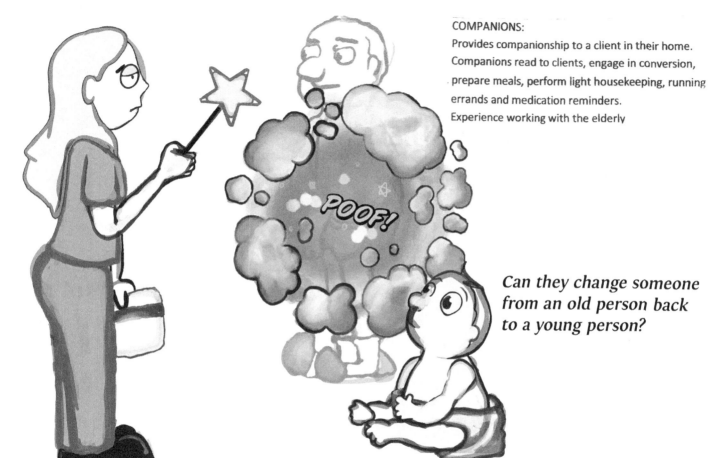

COMPANIONS:
Provides companionship to a client in their home. Companions read to clients, engage in conversion, prepare meals, perform light housekeeping, running errands and medication reminders.
Experience working with the elderly

POOF!

Can they change someone from an old person back to a young person?

Tallest turbines's blades stilled for servicing

Someone's
made
an
"S"
of
themself!

But it sounds like a holy ritual!

149

— An apparently "frazzled" mother left her 9-year-old daughter outside Richdale Convince Store on Main Street Thursday, ding police to report the

Just couldn't talk that kid into behaving!

step further—

████████, who wil entering his fourth season coaching the ████████ boys track program, takes the reigns as head coach of the entire program this spring. He split duties with

Are they making him king?

seeing many more seals.

"They're brutal," he said, "sneaking in under the net, ripping open the bellies of the cod; stealing lobsters right out of the pots. They opened 140 doors on my tarps in one day lat week."

Maybe you should try traps instead?

right, which she says decreases any bitter taste in the sauce. Then she chops the tomatoes into small pieces, and finely chops a spring of fresh basil to flavor the marinara

OR you could use a winter of oregano.

getting you the first word about the news that's happening in our home communities. But as this week's charter school and mosquito stories show, that first word is not the last — and it doesn't always paint the big picture.

As always, let me know that you think.

I AM, so therefore I MUST think.

Benefits:
- Compensation will be commiserate on experience.
- Health, 401k, paid holidays and vacation.

Maybe if they feel sorry for me,
they'll pay me more?

She said her father was sitting in the driver's seat, and with her being on the outside of the passenger's side, it was difficult for him to see what was happening. When he came around to her, he tried to shoe off the fox. When he would do so, it would run away but then

I've heard of Fox in Sox,* *but fox in shoes?!*

*Dr. Seuss, 1965

No. Your sex life should go on as before once you recover from the surgery. The desire to have sex and the ability to have organisms should also remain, despite the loss f ⸺ or ovaries. If sexual

Is that anything like bacteria?

"We appreciate all our local supermarkets and their commitment to this city," ▬▬▬▬ said. "Our sincere tanks to all those employees working to provide this service. Let's

An audit from 1981 reveals the department had 100 full-time workers; but that has been paired down to around 50 today, ▮▮▮ said. That only takes into consideration those

Yeah, but aren't 50 pairs 100 people?

level of the particular pond
is well beyond the control of
the applicant and any future
homeowners association, as it
rests with beavers that have
periodically damned the pond.
Beavers are a protected spe-

*Beavers may put curses on ponds,
but they're still protected!*

Baker: Fed tax reform may hit middle state's class hardest

Which one is the middle state?

9:53 p.m.: A driver was issued a criminal complaint and was summonsed to court for a stop sing violation and a suspended registration on

Must've been a really good song on the radio.

(MGA).

"I got connected with ▓▓▓ ▓▓▓ Golf through the ▓▓▓▓ Chamber of Commerce, then with the MGA as an off shute of my work with the magazine, and here I am in my 14th

Sounds dangerous; I'd want MY 'shute to be ON!

a **6:50 p.m.:** A person reported
l. a bike had been left in a poison
з ivy bush for months. Police
: decided to leave the bike in
the bush for the time being as
they did not want their officers
infected with poison ivy.

5:43 p.m.: Officers spoke with

Retrieval? Scratch THAT idea!

About the Illustrator

Ari Scott is a graphic artist from southern California. Her love for creativity and art started at the age of 10. Ari began pursuing art seriously in high school. During her time there she studied the history of fine arts, the fundamentals of art principles, multimedia painting, and figure drawing. Ari began exploring digital media in college. There she learned the fundamentals of design concept, logo design, color theory, and a plethora of other design principles. College helped sharpen her skill in Adobe Illustrator and Photoshop. Ari has obtained certifications in logo design, digital illustration, and digital advertising design.

About the Author

Susan M. "Sue" Lovett, a graduate of Bates College, is a freelance proofreader and copy editor. She began clipping anything and everything in print with humorous errors in choice of word, spelling, etc. when she was in high school (and we won't tell you how long ago THAT was!) and hasn't stopped since.

In high school she was awarded the English book prize and was voted "Class Bookworm" by her classmates. She is a former award-winning member of The International Save the Pun Foundation and continues to torture her friends to this day.

Made in the USA
Middletown, DE
19 July 2021